Brother Fire, Sister Earth

Brother Fire, Sister Earth

The Way of Francis of Assisi for
a Socially Responsible World

Adela DiUbaldo Torchia

NOVALIS

Layout and design: Gilles Lépine
Front cover: Francis of Assisi, St. Paul Cathedral, St. Paul, MN. Photo by
Gene Plaisted, OSC
© 1993 Novalis, Saint Paul University, Ottawa
Editorial office: Novalis, Saint Paul University, 223 Main Street, Ottawa,
Ontario K1S 1C4. Business office: Novalis, 49 Front Street East, 2nd Floor,
Toronto, Ontario M5E 1B3
Printed in Canada

Canadian Cataloguing in Publication Data

Torchia, Adela DiUbaldo, 1952-
    Brother fire, sister earth: the way of Francis of Assisi for
a socially responsible world

(Inner journey series)
Includes bibliographical references.
ISBN 2-89088-617-4

 1. Francis, of Assisi, Saint, 1182-1226
2. Spiritual life. 3. Christian saints —
Bibliography. I. Title. II. Series.

BX4700.F6T67   1993 271'.302 C93-090531-8

NOVALIS

Contents

For my father and mother,
Antonio and Concetta DiUbaldo

Preface

As we approach not only the end of this century but the end of the millennium as well, the need to retrieve those priceless pearls of wisdom from our past seems more critical than ever. In particular we might ask what or who, in the last thousand years of Christian history, continues to light our path as pilgrims and wayfarers through this world and towards the next.

Over eight centuries have passed since the birth of Francis of Assisi, but the transforming effect of his presence among us is still felt strongly by many who seek a role model to help them in their quest to love the Lord more dearly. Is the way of Francis of Assisi still relevant for our times? Or has our new focus on the social responsibility aspects of spirituality made him a useless relic?

The communications revolution in the twentieth century has made it almost impossible for us to plead ignorance about the sufferings of our fellow human beings, other creatures and the earth itself. As people of compassion we dare not shirk our responsibilities towards this reality of suffering in its many forms. And yet we often feel helpless in the face of the challenges before us, or exhausted from efforts that seem futile or unappreciated.

Francis embraced suffering as a means of stripping away the clutter of the heart so as to attain that inner freedom which allowed him to take such delight in the Lord. I hope you'll find the following pages transparent enough to let this exuberant "sun" of Assisi shine through.

I am much indebted, for my understanding of Francis, to Dr. Egil Grislis of the University of Manitoba, who imparted to me a lively sense of the treasures of the medieval mystics. I am also very grateful to my husband, Darryl Torchia, whose many patient rereadings of the text contributed much to its final format, and to my children, Elizabeth and Andrew, who have, along with Francis, taught me to take delight in the Lord.

Most scripture quotes are taken from the New Revised Standard Version of the Bible. And a small bibliography at the end of this text lists the most important works from which I have drawn my own understanding of Francis of Assisi and his relevance for our times.

1

The beginnings

During Francis of Assisi's lifetime (1181-1226), young men had many religious orders from which to choose. Francis, however, did not feel called to any of these but instead to a radically new form of religious life. The term "radical" comes from the latin "radix" meaning root. Usually we associate the term "radical" with something almost shockingly innovative and unheard of. Although the religious order that Francis eventually founded was radically new in its lifestyle approach (compared to most other religious orders in Europe at that time), it was also radical in the purer and seemingly opposite sense of going back to the roots of Christianity.

The other religious orders that existed in the Christian Europe of Francis' time had become well established as centres of charity, learning and prayer. The holiness of the original founders, and their followers' self-sacrifice and good intentions, prompted many people to donate what they could to support the work of these religious orders. Some donors left large bequests to support the monks' holy works in hopes that God would overlook some of the methods they had used to amass their wealth. This donated wealth was in turn used to help establish the main (in some cases, the only) schools and hospitals of the era.

At times, religious orders received donations of precious gems or other expensive artifacts to help finance their spiritual or apostolic works. These gifts, which initially came from people's admiration for the sanctity of the monasteries, eventually increased the orders' social status and property holdings. Francis fought against this tendency in his own order. Especially in the early years, he insisted that his followers must not allow themselves to become entrapped by the obligations and distractions of handling money and owning property. Today his prohibition against touching money may seem excessive, but his concern to remain unfettered to praise and serve God motivated his extreme caution. Francis, therefore, was unwilling to join any existing religious order since his vision of discipleship was so fundamentally different.

Discipleship

His vision was rooted in the way of life of Christ and the early church. This simple life, free from material preoccupations, was difficult for the Franciscans to maintain once they became better established. Nonetheless, Francis managed fairly well to hold up this radical ideal of the simple life without succumbing to the materialism so rampant in the well-established religious orders and the hierarchy of the Church of the time.

Francis is often dismissed in modern times as hopelessly simplistic in his approach to money and power. But I would argue that this is too harsh a judgment. He seemed to know how to avoid trouble with ecclesiastical authorities and survive in the Church while still retaining, living and inviting others to live his radical view of Christian discipleship. While others with similar goals were burned at the stake for condemning church triumphalism, Francis succeeded in calling people to a different way, a counter-cultural way, without allowing the difference to become abrasive and contentious. Nearly eight centuries later, we must shake our heads in admiration at his fascinating "sleight of hand."

Francis struggled to live the *vita apostolica* as Christ and the apostles had lived. His understanding of how they had lived was not free of short-sightedness, but it did gleam with a new freshness. Perhaps this was due to the ardour with which Francis and his early companions dared to turn their backs on lives of ease and comfort, pressing ahead instead to follow him who said, "Come, pick up your cross and follow me."

Ancient and traditional spiritualities, Christian and otherwise, stress that material things make intimacy with God difficult, if not impossible. Francis of Assisi's particular struggle to cast aside material concerns and live only for spiritual ones has captured the imagination of many over the centuries.

For a man so small of stature who lived so simply and wrote and travelled so little, Francis' far-reaching influence is phenomenal. Many authors take great liberties in depicting Francis according to their own most cherished or intriguing impressions. To some, Francis is God's fun-loving juggler; to others, he is a humourless, woman-hating ascetic.

In fact, not just authors, but many ordinary lay people have cherished rather peculiar images of St. Francis.

Francis' popularity is pervasive and extensive. Canonized only two years after his death, he attracted both men and women as followers. Some came to lead a celibate monastic life; others wanted to be Tertiari – married members of a Third Order – who would live in the world, taking care of their families and households while observing the Franciscan ideals of poverty and simplicity.

When a person of some means turns away from the comfortable life to pursue some nobler end, our attention is decidedly aroused. And turn away Francis did from the pleasant and comfortable life of the merchant's son. A party host par excellence, and a young man with a great zest for fashion, love songs and military honour, Francis became ill after his first attempt to gain fame as a chivalrous and gallant knight at arms. This illness stretched out into a prolonged melancholy. His life, hitherto so full of fun and promise, began to look jaded and empty. He broke dramatically from his fairly affluent life as a merchant's son, giving back to his father, who did not approve of this new direction in Francis' life, even the clothes he was wearing. Declaring that he was now espoused to Lady Poverty, Francis set out alone to determine how he might love and serve God with his whole being. In solitude and prayer he sought new nourishment for his spirit.

Discerning God's will

In the autumn of 1205, at the age of twenty-four, he heard a clear message coming from the crucifix at San Damiano: "Francis, go, repair my house, which, as you see, is falling completely to ruin." Four years later, when Francis petitioned Pope Innocent III to approve his religious order, he was at first dismissed. The pope later dreamed that the church was in danger of falling except for Francis, who acted as one of its supporting pillars. Shortly thereafter the Order of Friars Minor was officially founded.

But, in 1205, Francis had understood the message literally. He focussed on the crumbling walls of San Damiano, rather than the larger Church's need of healing and repair occasioned by the corruption of worldliness and power. So he set about, in spite of his inexperience, to repair the walls of San Damiano. Francis always started with the assumption that God was calling him to accomplish small things since he was so powerless and poor.

But perhaps God intended Francis' original understanding and response to be what it was. Here was a young man who may have had some overly romantic ideas about what it means to be poor. Whatever else it may mean, it almost always involves working with one's hands and one's back, growing food, cooking, mending old clothes, repairing houses and so on, even if one is not at all creatively inclined in these directions. And the sense of accomplishment that comes from reaping the harvest, from wearing the restored winter garment or from hearing winter winds howl outside the structure one has fortified with one's own hands cannot be measured. Pride may be a danger here, but that risk is surely outweighed by the sense of communion with nature and God that can come from restorative and creative work.

It might be safe to conjecture that while Francis' soft, aristocratic hands became raw and blistered rebuilding San Damiano, and his spirit enjoyed this new uncluttered relationship with God, his mind was subconsciously doing social theory. Dressed poorly against the cold, underfed and lifting heavy stones with his fragile body, Francis must have learned more about the life of the poor person than any amount of study would have revealed. The fact that he smiled at each privation does not mean that he did not feel it as a hardship; rather, he smiled because with each piled stone he left his old barren life further behind.

The rebuilding of San Damiano was not only a "hands-on" course in how the poor do things, it was also a visible and slow (due to Francis' inexperience) project which attracted the attention of his first followers. Just as a building's foundation may give no clue to the observer of the eventual structure that is to come, so Francis' actions did not register immediately on his watching friends. Little did they realize that the placement of each stone was slowly converting their hearts, thus allowing them to understand how much more important was Francis' project than their own wordly preoccupations.

Francis' most pressing concern, especially in the early days, was discerning God's plan for him and his rapidly increasing number of followers. Saint Bonaventure, Francis' most famous biographer, tells us that Francis wrestled valiantly with the temptation to live a life of contemplation only. He considered himself too uneducated and inexperienced to preach, and more drawn to prayer. But Francis reluctantly concluded that "it seems . . . more in accordance with God's will that I should renounce the peace of contemplation and go out to work." So he decided to attend to the people's spiritual and physical needs by preaching God's word and by toiling side by side with the poor to earn his daily bread.

Francis loved the earth and cared deeply about the well-being of all creatures. His compassion stretched beyond a concern for the sufferings of humans to include the sufferings of animals. Whenever possible, Francis freed trapped animals and even threw caught fish back in the water if they were still alive. Clearly, Francis' orientation was not so exclusively other-wordly that he failed to notice the society and world around him. He took to heart the demands of compassion that Jesus himself imposed upon his followers and fulfilled with his life.

Francis always tried to ensure that his heart had plenty of room for God, and, though he considered himself unworthy of it, he knew on many occasions that God was graciously using his talents despite the fact that they were so small and insignificant. To be alienated or treated with contempt is another form of poverty, and many deeply wounded people in the Church today are devoted to this saint who knew how to survive rejection, and how to love Jesus in spite of all the Church's human flaws.

An apparent contradiction

Francis had a certain innocence about him and he took a childlike delight in all of creation. But simple he was not! On the contrary, he and his alliance with Lady Poverty are quite complex. The *Omnibus of Sources*, which lists the books, articles and commentaries devoted to Francis, contains almost two thousand pages and grows with each new edition. No saint has had more biographers (secular and ecclesiastical) or supporters holding completely contradictory views of the man. This would belie Francis' simplicity. Authentic spirituality and the demands of compassion seem to pull in apparently opposite directions: 1) towards a more intense and exclusive relationship with God, and 2) towards a more fervent and active concern for the suffering of others. Yet Francis managed this tension well and his balance pole was poverty.

Many people who are perhaps naively attracted to Francis (for instance because of "his" peace prayer which actually cannot be traced back beyond the early twentieth century) are shocked to learn of some of the extremes to which he carried his campaign to root out all other tastes and affections within himself other than a taste and affection for God. In his *First Life*, Thomas Celano, a disciple and contemporary of Francis, wrote: "He [Francis] used to say it is impossible to satisfy necessity and not give in to pleasure. Cooked foods he permitted himself scarcely at all or very rarely; and if he did allow them, he either mixed them with ashes or destroyed their flavour with cold water" (1 Celano 51). If Francis found himself a guest at a sumptuous meal, "he would taste a bit of the meat in observance of the holy Gospel [Luke 10:8] and then, making a pretense of eating by raising his hand to his mouth, lest anyone should perceive what he was doing, he would drop the rest in his lap" (1 Celano 51).

When young children resort to such deception and wastefulness to get rid of foods they do not want to eat, praise for their sanctity seldom follows! Francis, of course, was not throwing away these foods because he disliked their taste, but one wonders whether a simple "No, thank you, I've already eaten" would not have sufficed! The servants who swept the floor after such a banquet no doubt appreciated the treat, but I wonder what they thought of this holy and virtuous act?

In Celano's *Second Life*, a certain brother has a vision of Francis immediately after Francis' death. In the vision, he sees Francis in heaven enjoying a welcoming banquet with his brother friars, "and he began to eat happily with them at a table prepared most splendidly and filled with many delicious foods" (2 Celano 219). If an occasional sumptuous meal is a sinful thing on earth, why would there be such things in heaven? We are led to question either Francis' sanity (or at least good sense) or Celano's lack of self-restraint in embellishing Francis' sanctity. Of course, early biographers such as Celano had no idea that their penchant for exaggeration would elicit scorn rather than praise from future generations of Christians.

A counter-cultural model

How can Francis of Assisi help us on our own spiritual quest in the late twentieth century? There is no easy answer to this question. In many ways Francis goes totally against the grain of our society's values. Francis did not think of himself as number one. He did not believe that he deserved the best, except, of course, the best that is Christ. He sought always to reduce his bodily needs and cravings, in accordance with the classical wisdom of all great religions, rather than to gratify them. How can we today understand someone who deliberately chose "the lesser" of everything for himself? And, more importantly, how can we speak of the immense joy it gave him to choose the lesser? These are questions our culture may not have the vocabulary to answer.

In the face of those who deliberately seek out the smaller, shabbier portions for themselves, our cultural (and psychological) vocabulary offers labels like masochist, pessimist, defeatist or misfit. Counselling is usually recommended to redirect this person towards a more "positive" self-image. How does this outlook fit with the wisdom of the Crucified?

In accepting the cross, Jesus accepted the way of hardship and pain. His anguish in the Garden of Gethsemane makes it impossible for us to overlook the reality of the conscious choice he made. We can only assume, from his agonizing at this point, that he could have chosen to escape from pain and humiliation. Only when he truly accepted his cross did the drama leading through crucifixion to resurrection begin to unfold. Love for us led Jesus to accept pain and humiliation. He entered completely into the human condition, even accepting to die as all humans must.

At the beginning of his ministry Jesus felt the necessity of preparing himself by fasting in the desert for forty days. Jesus' asceticism is often downplayed (though Francis did not do so) in an affluent society that prefers to hear that his yoke is easy and his burden is light. But this saying was addressed to the "heavily laden" or "heavily burdened" (Matthew 11:28-30), a fact too many of us tend conveniently to forget. Francis found Jesus' yoke neither easy nor light, but he did find that it fit well and he wore it as best he could.

Jesus had a high-pressure "salesperson" working on him to choose the easy and light way right at the end of his forty days in the wilderness (Matthew 4:1-11). Knowing the physical hunger with which Jesus' human body must have been racked, the Tempter encouraged him to change the stones into bread. Why not? Many people today ask the same thing. If God is good, and so many people are starving, why doesn't God feed them . . . change the stones into bread? Why should we change our lifestyles, for instance, by eating less meat to free up more grain to feed hungry people instead of cattle?

The all-powerful God could take care of this problem with a proverbial wave of the hand. Instead God merely provides an earth capable of sustaining vast millions more than are presently sustained, and lets us choose how to use it or abuse it, whether to share it or just to grab the best and the most. But as Jesus told the Tempter, we do not live by bread alone, but by every word that comes from the mouth of God. In particular he later pointed out two "words," the two most important commandments: to love God with one's whole heart and soul and strength, and to love one's neighbour as oneself. So Jesus did not turn the stones into bread, but instead preached a message of love designed to turn our hearts of stone into hearts of flesh.

Francis chose to become one with those who suffered from hunger by sharing their experience of lacking everything but God. Did Francis, then, feel that caring for and helping the poor was not an important job? Clearly this is not so since he himself came to rely on the generosity of others for survival. He believed so strongly in this generosity that he discouraged his followers from storing food and supplies for the morrow. Each day the friars minor were to beg alms of the faithful while they tried to live and reveal the reality of God's gracious presence as an answer to deeper human hungers.

As we rush headlong towards the third millennium, generally exhausting ourselves on the treadmill of keeping up appearances, we might do well to look for the lonely figure of Francis of Assisi on the horizon, bearing his alms bowl, walking towards us. For a few crumbs of our attention, he might just touch us with his contagious and exuberant love for the Lord!

Can the example of Francis of Assisi, the restorer of San Damiano's crumbling walls, help us restore the crumbling faith of Christians in a secular age? Let us not underestimate the power of seemingly insignificant people doing apparently unimportant jobs. God seemed to use Francis' very insistence on remaining a "lesser" or "minor" to accomplish some astonishing things.

2

Francis as mystic

The love of nature and poverty

In the last few years, I have enjoyed my most sublime moments of prayer on the eastern shore of Lake Winnipeg. Whether watching the sunset, or listening to the rhythmic heartbeat of the waves rising and falling, I felt God's nearness. Even to look at the lake when it is simply still and mirror-like is an experience of having the work of the Creator reflected into my life. The opening words of Psalm 19 strike a deep chord of resonance: "The heavens declare the glory of God, the vault of heaven proclaims God's handiwork; day discourses of it to day, night to night hands on the knowledge."

Perhaps the greatest link that I feel with Francis of Assisi is our common love of nature. I think he would understand what it's like to sit mesmerized by the beauty of some ancient rock or dying leaf, or to feel the nervous rush in my being quieted by the sudden nearness of a bird or squirrel or fox. Even in the city, while driving through rush-hour traffic with a car full of noisy, arguing passengers, I am suddenly lifted away into a world of beauty, grace and peace by gazing at the colours of the evening sky.

Many writers say that nature is the prime example of the symbolic and sacramental in our lives. Nature provides a peephole, as it were, into the eternal. I remember learning as a child that the intricate geometric design of each snowflake is unique. No two snowflakes are exactly alike! To me this amazing diversity and infinite variety in something as mundane as snow was proof of God's existence. And thirty years later, after studying many philosophical and theological systems of proofs for God's existence, the lowly snowflake still seems to offer more conclusive evidence that a loving, intelligent and beautiful Creator has masterminded every detail of this universe we call home.

So even an insignificant gem of nature like the snowflake can be a symbol of the eternal; and when such a thing moves us to meditate on the presence of God in creation, it takes on the sacramental function of making visible God's grace in our midst. Saint Augustine spoke of the existence of a wide range of "sacramentals." Perhaps our lowly snowflake, which is here one moment and melted against our coat the next, is one such sacramental – a concrete, physical reality that points to the presence of God in our midst.

Respect nature

To feel God's presence and nearness is surely to experience grace in its most celebrative form. To feel this nearness acutely is the experience of the mystic. Francis, therefore, is known as a nature mystic. His biographer and companion, Thomas of Celano, wrote that, in every work of the artist, Francis praised the Artist. He saw the beauty of creation as a ladder that led up to the Creator. Shortly before his death, while lying ill in the convent of the Poor Clares at his beloved

San Damiano, Francis wrote a poem in praise of creation with the explicit intention of inspiring people to be less offensive to God in their relationship with creation. And we thought ecology was a twentieth-century concern! Here is Francis' famous "Canticle to Brother Sun":[1]

Most high, all-powerful, all good, Lord!
All praise is yours, all glory, all honour
And all blessing.

To you, alone, Most High, do they belong.
No mortal lips are worthy
To pronounce your name.

All praise be yours, my Lord,
through all that you have made,
And first my lord Brother Sun,

How beautiful is he, how radiant in all his splendour!
Of you, Most High, he bears the likeness.

All praise be yours, my Lord,
through Sister Moon and Stars;
In the heavens you have made them, bright
And precious and fair.

All praise be yours, my Lord,
through Brothers Wind and Air,
And fair and stormy, all the weather's moods,
By which you cherish all that you have made.

All praise be yours, my Lord, through Sister Water,

---

1. Francis of Assisi. *Writings and Early Biographies: English Omnibus of Sources for the Life of St. Francis.* Translated by Benen Fahy. Edited by Marion Habig. (Chicago: Franciscan Herald, 1983), pp. 130-131.

So useful, lowly, precious and pure.

All praise be yours, my Lord, through Brother Fire,
through whom you brighten up the night.
How beautiful is he, how gay!
Full of power and strength.

All praise be yours, my Lord,
through Sister Earth, our mother,
Who feeds us in her sovereignty and produces
Various fruits with coloured flowers and herbs.

All praise be yours, my Lord,
through those who grant pardon for love of you;
through those who endure sickness and trial.

Happy those who endure in peace,
By you, Most High, they will be crowned.

All praise be yours, my Lord, through Sister Death,
From whose embrace no mortal can escape.

Woe to those who die in mortal sin!
Happy those she finds doing your will!
The second death can do no harm to them.

Praise and bless my Lord, and give him thanks,
And serve him with great humility.

Francis' relevance for contemporary ecological concerns
lies in his great respect for nature which is clearly evident in
the above canticle. This canticle reflects something else as
well, Francis' general attitude of "stepping lightly on the
earth."

Obviously, Francis was not concerned about the ozone layer, the greenhouse effect, the destruction of the rain forests, or acid rain. These problems clearly did not exist in thirteenth-century Europe. So what motivated Francis to step so lightly on the earth? I believe that he had an inner sense of the mind – and spirit-polluting effects of over-consumption; and he also had so profound a respect for all creation that he found the unnecessary slaughter of any creature abhorrent.

More with less

The parental admonition not to snack before dinner to avoid "spoiling your appetite" is a familiar one. To indulge a child's craving for junk-food is to dull her hunger for the nourishment of the well-prepared meal. When the child rebels against the admonition with "But I'm hungry," the parent can reply: "Good, you'll enjoy your dinner then." As adult people of faith, do we dare to apply this same understanding to our hunger for God? To hunger for God is often considered an exercise best left to the capable hearts of mystics. But there is little chance of our experiencing much depth in the divine-human encounter unless we allow ourselves to feel this hunger for God. Perhaps Francis of Assisi understood that, as we purge ourselves of excessive appetites, we can nurture a hunger for God.

Purging the body of excessive appetites fits in well with Francis' conviction about the importance of poverty. To live intimately with God, Francis took Lady Poverty as his spiritual spouse. He felt that only by continually embracing her could he fruitfully serve God with his whole being.

As a merchant's son, Francis was generous; he treated his friends to good times, and he gave alms to the poor who came to beg in the shop. When his father was away, as he often was on extended buying trips, Francis was especially generous to these beggars. And then the sparks would fly when his father came back and took inventory of sales and receipts. Even after his original vision and message from the crucified Christ at San Damiano, Francis still relied on his father's wealth to sponsor his philanthropic projects. When he sold a bolt of his father's cloth to get the money for bricks and mortar for repairing San Damiano, his enraged father no doubt pointed out that, since Francis had no interest in carrying on the family business, he ought not to depend on the profits of that business to sponsor the simple and holy life that he now craved.

Fearfully hiding in San Damiano from his father's anger, which had been steadily increasing over the last few years, Francis gained a new perspective on the use of money. He realized that he would never be free to love and serve the Lord completely unless he could get away from needing money. He required a small amount of the simplest and cheapest foods to stay alive, but this need could be met through begging alms. In seeing how much freedom he could gain from living on very little or even no money, Francis was a precursor of those who now espouse the "more-with-less" philosophy to counter excessive consumerism. (We will deal with this more thoroughly in Chapter four.)

Francis' lifelong aim (after his profound conversion experience) was to get rid of all affections, attachments and dependencies other than Christ. Some of the extremes he embraced to accomplish this may seem rather scandalous to our relatively pampered age. For instance, he mixed ashes with his food so that he would not crave to eat too much, and he threw himself naked into the snow to quell certain passions that stubborn "Brother Ass" (his name for his body) refused to abandon.

But these things were not done in a spirit of meanness or masochism. "Few things are needed, in fact, only one," Jesus said to Martha of Bethany, who was worrying and fretting about so many things (Luke 10:41). But Brother Ass seemed to "need" so many things with such urgency. So Francis decided to wage war on these many needs so he could better live with his heart, according to Jesus' advice to Martha. To do this he embraced a life of austerity and self-denial.

Poverty and asceticism

Francis refused to criticize people for mishandling funds that might have been directed towards the poor. Instead, by "wedding" Lady Poverty he became poor himself, in fact the poorest of the poor, always being careful not to have anything himself that someone else might lack. Francis' horizon was not as broad as our own. He saw no film footage of starving children, overworked mothers and despairing fathers in poor countries. But he did see the poverty in his own country and he always gave away whatever he had been given to help others in need.

Some people today criticize Francis because he did not speak up in favour of social justice issues. But this is rather unfair. Francis' way of living spoke volumes about the Christian duty of compassion towards the suffering. By becoming one with the poor, he drew attention to their plight, and left the Holy Spirit in charge of "appropriate spectator response." As it is written in the first letter of John (3:17): "How does God's love abide in anyone who has the world's goods and sees a brother or sister in need and yet refuses to help?" For Francis, compassion was the only acceptable response to the great suffering which many of God's creatures endured. Indeed, compassion should be an automatic response, as far as Francis was concerned.

For this reason Francis avoided confrontational tactics to arouse human compassion. When a certain doctor of theology pressed him to explain how he could remain quiet and uncritical when others were living selfish, sinful lives, Francis hesitated to respond. The learned doctor referred to God's warning to the prophet, in Ezekiel 3:18, to prove the necessity of exposing people's sins to them: "If I say to the wicked, 'You shall surely die,' and you give them no warning, or speak to warn the wicked from their wicked way, in order to save their life, those wicked persons shall die for their iniquity; but their blood I will require at your hand." Francis answers that the life of God's humble servant shines so brilliantly that others cannot help but notice and, in the appropriate cases, be put to shame.

The learned doctor was apparently much impressed although Francis' answer could be seen, especially today, as almost too simple. But I believe that Francis' "simple" answer was deceptively complex. He was in fact telling us that, although it goes against human nature to smile kindly at those who do not make the sacrifices we make in serving God, we cannot hope to arouse them with criticism, if we have not been able to inspire them with example.

Only towards his own friars was Francis openly critical in pointing out the demands of faith. For the rest of humanity, he preferred to point at the truth that, since God's love is for all creatures, the poor and suffering must not be neglected. If his "pointing" was sometimes imprecise, Francis knew that the Holy Spirit could easily be consulted for further directions.

As we know, Francis' own friars were constrained to a life of poverty and asceticism. Asceticism, a lifestyle of austerity and self-denial, has had a very checkered history in Christian thinking. As early as the fifth century, Saint Augustine found himself waging an intense battle against the monk Pelagius, who seemed to be preaching that human beings could earn God's favour by their virtuous acts and religious lifestyles. In a certain sense, the sixteenth-century Protestant Reformation was also about this same controversy, as have been a number of other theological disagreements over the centuries. The pendulum has swung many times between the pole of human arrogance (thinking we can merit salvation) and human laziness (leaving everything to God since grace and salvation are gifts). One wonders whether the current North American disdain for any form of self-sacrifice reiterates the ancient Christian truth that our behaviour cannot merit God's freely given gift of grace. Or is it just an excuse to be selfish?

But Francis seemed unconcerned about earning or not earning grace. He wanted to live and hunger only for God. Other hungers, wants and cravings had to be subdued, or crushed if necessary, to make room. Having slowly and painfully come to the knowledge that making God the centre of one's existence brought immeasurable joy and peace, Francis wanted to help others away from the ignorance that kept them bound to things of the flesh. In this focus on removing peripheral human desires to rid life of illusions that blind us to the nearness of the eternal, Francis' way has much in common with the "middle way" of the Buddhist eightfold path. And in the spirit of interreligious dialogue, I will examine this interesting connection in Chapter five. But first, let us examine whether Francis' brand of asceticism has any relevance for us today.

3

Franciscan asceticism

A paradox for our times

When we speak of the relevance of the way of Francis for our own times, we dare not pass over the subject of his asceticism too hastily. Asceticism is out of style now, and its enemies claim that there is really no difference between it and masochism. Masochism, of course, is a pathological condition in which one deliberately seeks out pain and suffering for oneself. A healthy asceticism, born out of a yearning for God, is the opposite: it is the attempt to remove the great variety of distractions that hinder our progress along the path to God.

Advertisers work hard to convince us that we *need* so many things to be happy. We need the right clothes, the right body, the right skin, the right hair and so forth. We need to drink the right beverages and consume the right foods. We need to drive the right cars and shop in the right places. Our children need to have the right toys and clothes and bikes.

We need to keep changing the furniture in our homes and match the floor coverings and walls to get "the country look" or "the sophisticated look" or whatever is the latest trend.

Of course, to fulfil all these needs we must seek out the most high-paying job possible. We must study disciplines that will open the doors to these jobs. Many people consider the study of religion, music, philosophy, art or the humanities foolish unless they can be made to fit into the public school curriculum which is designed largely to prepare young people for the job market. This curriculum therefore contains less and less of those subjects that nourish the human spirit, and more and more of those subjects which are geared towards economic production and profit. Students still study poetry and other literature because learning to communicate well, to use the language well, is an important tool in "business." But even these subjects are not secure in a world that continually asks: How is this going to help me get a job?

The classical questions about the meaning and purpose of our existence have been replaced by such things as guidebooks on how to write resumés. Career counselling consists almost exclusively of videos, workshops and computer programs designed to pinpoint job skills and formulate "career goals" to fit into the world of business. We need no longer wonder about existence, since its meaning and purpose are clear: to get a high-paying office job in the business world.

In the typical North American family both parents must work full-time to pay for all those many, many things that are "needed"; and the baby, therefore, is awakened at dawn (earlier in winter) from the time that the maternity benefits expire, usually when the infant is about three months old, and bundled into the car to be taken to the babysitter's for the day and for most of the week. Progressive parents are reassured by their babysitters that the infant will not be "spoiled" by being picked up when she or he just perversely wants attention. If their diaper is dry and they have been fed, then they will stay in their baby seat, which can be tilted a little when they stop crying and finally fall asleep until the next diaper change or feeding becomes necessary. Mom and Dad can rest assured that their infant will learn early that it's no use crying because no one will come by and pick you up. Like the priest and the Levite they will walk on the other side of the road or room. I wonder how Jesus feels about this, Jesus who scolded his apostles when they tried to prevent children from "bothering" him?

When Mom and Dad (if Dad's still around!) get home from work, they are exhausted and they have so much to do. In the two or three hours between their homecoming and junior's bedtime there's dinner to make, laundry to do, sometimes a trip to the store. Perhaps the car needs attention or one parent has a course or a lesson to get to, or another family member needs help with something. Mom and Dad are not usually in a very receptive mood in these two or three hours because they really do have too much to do and they really are too tired. If they do take some time to relax it's most likely in front of the television, which, even if they are sitting with their child, leaves something to be desired in terms of the quality of their presence.

But it won't be long before children are old enough to understand why it has to be this way. Once they realize that all the colour co-ordinated furniture and carpeting and drapery in their nice big houses and their late model new car(s) and all the other expensive things in their lives are absolute necessities, they will surely forgive their parents' continual business, absenteeism and fatigue. If this forgiveness is a bit slow in coming, the parents usually initiate the children as quickly as possible into becoming voracious consumers themselves so that their happiness, by age three or so, also depends on getting the right things from the toy department and eating food in the right places that hand out colourful plastic prizes to the children while they eat.

Just say no

Compared to the rat-race kind of existence that the average North American family endures today, the followers of Francis had it easy. And that is exactly what Francis' message is for us today: *be easier on yourselves and each other and the earth!*

Step lightly! Travel as pilgrims on the journey of life. Carry and possess as little as possible. Re-evaluate your needs. The more things you need, the less free you are. Asceticism is not masochism! Asceticism means saying no to all the things that claim to be crucial for your happiness but which in fact are a burden and a distraction. At first there's a lot of pain involved in this – you perhaps wear clothes that are a bit frumpy and frayed, or you make an effort to consume fewer of your fellow creatures as food, or you forego trips in favour of charity or learning – you don't fit in, you're a misfit. People resent you even if you voice no criticism of their lifestyles. And they will interpret your refusal to participate in the general "getting and spending" as a negative judgement of their behaviour.

People who have tried to reduce their needs in this way have found that maintaining good relations isn't always easy. If you are fasting at the same table with others who are feasting, you must be extra cheerful, extra solicitous and extra kind. Then and only then will they forgive you for not needing what they need.

Train hard

Step lightly! Step lightly on each other. Francis demanded a lot from his followers. Just change the "sc" in asceticism to "thl" and you have athleticism. Do people criticize or praise athletes who exert themselves to the limit, who perhaps abuse their bodies with rigour and discipline to win the race or beat the record time? Usually, praise is the more common reaction for athletes who push themselves to the limit. But when people push themselves to the limit by practising an asceticism designed to train their bodies, minds and hearts to find joy in serving Christ, they are condemned as fanatics. It's apparently okay to be religious about athletics but not okay to be religious about religion!

To step lightly, to make it look easy and fun, you have to train hard. Francis was the Olympic coach par excellence. He loved his brother friars with a tender passion. The early biographers report that he asked the friars to call him "mother." And yet, because he loved them, he could not endure seeing them still enslaved to the things of this world. He knew that Christ had freed them and meant them to remain free. Just as a mother eventually weans her children from the breast on which they had relied for survival so that they might enter a more mature level of existence, so, too, Francis treated his friars with high expectations as well as warmth and affection. He let them have few things, but he let them have himself. He had time for them.

Respect nature

Step lightly! The third aspect of Francis' way of stepping lightly was to respect the earth and his fellow creatures. Francis clearly avoided overconsumption like the plague that it has become for our times. He practised the three "r's" with rigour. He *reduced* his needs to the barest minimum. He *reused* his one outfit of clothing and any other "things" he used day after day for most of his adult life. He *recycled* in the most creative ways. He even recycled "live meat," animals destined for the cooking fire, into free creatures again by turning them loose. And he used old cloaks that others had thrown out as his only winter covering until he came across someone who seemed to need the cloak more than he did, and then he recycled it again, into *their* winter covering.

Francis stepped lightly on the earth because creation was a glorious manifestation of the Creator. His reverence for nature was quite unique among Christian saints – and only 750 years ahead of his time! People laughed at Francis because he preached to the birds. Perhaps the birds are still God's freest and most musical creatures partly because they have passed on, from one generation to the next, Francis' message that their Creator is obviously very good.

Get rid of distractions

Franciscan asceticism applied to our times is not something to groan at but something to sing about. Gabriel Marcel, the twentieth-century Christian philosopher, argues that every time we give in to ourselves we may unawares be laying an additional limitation on ourselves, forging our own chain. So Francis' dual message of "be easy on yourselves" and "be willing to give up all for Christ" is paradoxical, but not contradictory. A famous passage from the letter to the Hebrews reminds us that the life of the Christian is an active life: "Therefore, since we are surrounded by so great a cloud of witnesses, let us also lay aside every weight . . . and let us run with perseverance the race that is set before us . . ." (Hebrews 12:1).

The alarm rings at 5:45 and the race is on. Back in the bedroom at 6:06 – good, my showers are taking less time. A blessed hour of peaceful reading over coffee and toast and then the race is on again. Drag two kids out of bed, yell at them to hurry into the kitchen, make two breakfasts and two lunches at the same time, complain to husband about not being able to cope. While driving my daughter to 7:30 a.m. basketball practice because it is still dark, I see men and women emerging from cars carrying full baby seats and dragging sleepy two-year-olds through deep, snowy boulevards. Rush and push, rush and push – the day goes on like this, and then the evening, and then the next day: "What do people gain from all the toil at which they toil under the sun? A generation goes and a generation comes, but the earth remains forever. The sun rises and the sun goes down, and hurries to the place where it rises" (Ecclesiastes 1:3-5).

The ancient Hebrew writers of the book of Ecclesiastes seemed to penetrate the heart of the matter with these perceptive words. Who says the Bible is irrelevant to hectic modern times? "The sun rises and the sun goes down, and hurries to the place where it rises." This may be astronomically incorrect (it far predates Galileo), but the sharpness and validity of its ongoing social commentary is astounding. With such simple words and the simplest of images, it captures the futility of our distracted lives. What is it that we're trying to gain with all our toil? What is the prize for which we run the race? What do we hope to receive from the Lord? Better still – *how* – how can we receive from the Lord, when our hands and our hearts are so full?

As a young adult Francis made the decision to "lay aside every weight," to throw off everything that hinders. Rejecting the life of material security that could have been his, he devoted himself to a life of asceticism instead, trying to solve this one problem – how to receive from the Lord? He continually strove to empty his hands and heart so that he might receive, not just this or that bauble or trinket, not even grace, forgiveness or salvation (words Francis seldom used), but rather God alone. Nothing else was good enough. Everything else fell short. As Augustine had said before him: "Our hearts are restless until they rest in thee."

Asceticism has often been misunderstood as "adding on" instead of "subtracting from" the demands made on our lives. To do without certain conveniences or luxuries, or to "live more simply" seems to take so much more work and time and energy. And yet, in some mysterious way, the simpler and poorer life seems to contain more space for receiving from the

Lord. This is another paradox "for the wisdom of this world is foolishness for God" (1 Corinthians 3:19) but "God's foolishness is wiser than human wisdom" (1 Corinthians 1:25).

Catholic Christians have often been chided about their willingness to be satisfied with "well, it's a mystery" when religious questions seem impossible to resolve. But is this really something to be embarrassed about? I think not, since any faith that has all the answers is quite simply a contradiction in terms: there is no need of faith when every answer is known. Francis actually prided himself on knowing very little. He spent most of his short adult life, for example, just trying to draw closer to Jesus. Sometimes he felt drawn to the Lord in a sublime and totally private intimacy about which we can only speculate. Other times, his faith was very public, and he preached at length about God's desire to share our lives, with all their burdens and hopes.

This push and pull of the divine-human encounter has been noted by a number of authors. "God says come, God says go," writes contemporary liberation theologian Leonardo Boff, in speaking of the necessity for both prayer and action in the authentic life of faith. Removing some of the distractions in our lives generally makes us more able to receive from the Lord. But the gift of God's grace, once received, must be used and shared. In trying to understand the mystery of this push and pull that Francis and so many other Christians have experienced, I found myself poetically exploring the deeper mystery of who Jesus is:

"He is my song," the badge said,
How lovely – the thought gives me wings,
I hear a flute, a lilting melody,
The sound of summer breezes rustling leaves . . .

But Jesus is also the reality of human anguish.
Taking walks on summer evenings,
Through open windows hearing

Families fighting, parents shouting,
Children crying . . .

Children hungry for love,
Peeking through fence slats
At happy families laughing together in the sunlight.
Look into the eyes of these hungry children
    and see Jesus crucified,
No longer able to bear the taunts
Of a humanity unable to accept his love.

"He is my song . . ."
The husband's tender glance cast towards
    his silent weeping wife across the room,
Bright orange evening sunlight
After a whole day of unbroken gloom . . .
This is Jesus,
A father dancing with his newborn son.

The mystery of Jesus . . .
God revealed for you and me.
A God who weeps for Lazarus, his friend,
A God who rages at human greed and indifference,
A God who bleeds on the cross, heart pierced with pain.

I have made Jesus so human at times,
Wanting to touch him,
Needing him to touch me,
A person among persons, a friend among friends,
Too human, yes I've done that,
Made him two sizes too small, like me.

Others say he did not really suffer, only pretended,
God inside a human shell,
Nothing to fear,
He read the script beforehand,
Went through the motions, pretended anguish,
But he was God,

And God is not afraid of things,
God doesn't cry, doesn't get angry,
        doesn't sweat blood in Thursday evening gardens,
But Jesus did,
And he was God, still is.

Jesus is the paradox of the Beatitudes,
Thirsting for justice, yet not angry, bringing peace,
Gentle and merciful, yet persecuted, misunderstood,
Jesus is hope where hope is illogical,
He is found in the heights of our joys
And in the depths of our sorrows.
But always, wherever we see him,
He calls us to hope,
Calls us to compassionate mercy.

Jesus is merciful love in a world so ruled
        by merciless hate and the desire to dominate.
Jesus is the agonizing pain of labour changed in one
        overwhelming instant to the joy of birth.
Jesus is the glint of joy in the eyes of the handicapped
        so unburdened as they are of all that weighs
        on the minds of the strong, so many problems to solve.
Jesus answers them without solutions, with no conclusions,
Jesus answers them so clearly, with love.

The mystery of Jesus . . .
Calling us out of ourselves to the other,
Calling us away from the other, to himself,
Calling us to share with those in need,
Calling us to celebrate what we have,
Calling us to be cautious about our strengths
        and to exalt, instead, in our brokenness,
Calling us again to celebrate our strengths,
        and to fear all that which holds us back.

But calling us, always calling our names,
Calling us forth, calling us back,

The way is mysterious but not dark . . .
The mystery of Jesus,
His love frees me and my freedom carries me away,
The mystery of Jesus, smiling, waiting for my return.

I believe that Francis felt this ongoing pull and push of God, calling him forth to work and share and love, and calling him back to receive rest and renewal, to be restored to life, ultimately to be resurrected into an eternal life of intimacy with God.

But Francis did not have all the answers. He was often quiet when people wanted him to speak. And he spent a lot of time quietly observing the reality of God's presence in the life of all creatures, both in their joys and in their sorrows. Francis never became a priest. Perhaps, and this is purely speculation on my part, the presence of Christ in the eucharist, great as it was, was still so limited.

Who are you Jesus?
Have I made you too much like what I need you to be?
I pray that at times I have let you be you.
Thank you for accepting me as I am,
And thank you for loving me too much to leave me there.

Just say yes . . . to the Lord

Francis of Assisi is seldom viewed as a tireless social activist. He shared his bread to the point of going hungry, but he seemed more interested in conquering himself, with his asceticism, than in overcoming various social ills. In this he was a product of his time. He knew his place. He knew how quickly, for one thing, his tired and frail bones could become kindling for the heretic's fire if his message was interpreted as critical of the powers that be. He raised up the poor by making himself their equal or lesser. Once the poor had become visible, the individual Christian, guided by the Holy Spirit, could decide how to respond.

Many modern Christians dismiss the medieval mystics, and other heroes of Christian asceticism, because they want to have *more* in life, not *less*. Why suffer when God is a God of joy and abundance? Why sacrifice when Christ made the ultimate sacrifice for us, once and for all? Why should we practise austerity and deny ourselves when we are the blessed children of Almighty God? God, our all-loving parent, wants us to be happy and free.

But who is "us"? Clearly none of us here on this earth is God's only child. No person, no group, no church can claim exclusive rights to the love of so great a God. As human parents we are saddened when some children suffer need, while others squander what might have been used to meet that need. We cannot claim that God's wisdom coincides with this foolish human wisdom. But can we tolerate an image of God that is indifferent to the sufferings of "one of the least of these who are members of my family" (Mt 25:40)? We do not claim to know God, but we do know that that God is "more" than we are – more loving, more caring, more compassionate, more just and more merciful.

Before so compassionate and merciful a God, then, do we dare to be petty and selfish? Or do we follow Francis' example in saying no to ourselves, striving "to enter through the narrow door" (Lk 13:24) so that we can say yes to the Lord? The paradox of asceticism – that we cannot receive from the Lord with hands and hearts already full – is "a mystery we can cling to." This is the more-with-less of the gospels – Jesus promising us more joy and peace than we can imagine, if we are willing to become less and less. The grain of wheat must fall into the ground and die if it is to bear fruit. Jesus himself took the challenge seriously and "emptied himself, taking the form of a slave; . . . he humbled himself and became obedient to the point of death, death on a cross" (Philippians 2:7-8).

Since we are dealing in paradoxes, we turn now to the paradox that Francis lived so well – the Beatitudes.

4

More with less

Francis and the Beatitudes

Francis was a man of the Beatitudes. The spirit of the Beatitudes infused his whole approach to life and God and others. The Beatitudes guided Francis in his spiritual life. Indeed, when examined in light of Francis' way, the Beatitudes can take on new meaning for our own efforts at balancing spirituality with social responsibility.

The Beatitudes are the more-with-less philosophy of the gospels. This makes them especially relevant to our observations about how the way of Francis fits in so well with a new "ecology" of the spiritual life. In each of the Beatitudes, Jesus celebrates a situation of "less," like being poor or meek or in mourning or persecuted, and points out the great potential for the "more," if these situations are lived out with courage.

In the more-with-less philosophy of physical ecology, we are invited to the "more" of healthier living, and better prospects for the future of our earth and its resources, by consuming less, discarding less and learning to enjoy living with less. Seeking and living with fewer material things also makes our lives a more fertile ground for the cultivation of spiritual values. Since this was Francis' approach, let us see how the Beatitudes can help us to understand the validity of Francis' way for today.

The importance of poverty

The Beatitudes appear in both Matthew's and Luke's gospels. The shorter version of the Beatitudes in Luke ends with a series of "woes" that could easily have helped trigger the conversion that Francis underwent: "But woe to you who are rich, for you have received your consolation. Woe to you who are full now, for you will be hungry. Woe to you who are laughing now, for you will mourn and weep. Woe to you when all speak well of you, for that is what their ancestors did to the false prophets" (Luke 6:24-26). Hearing this gospel passage proclaimed at mass, Francis may well have reflected on how aptly it described his life as a merchant's son. He certainly never went hungry and he was very popular among his friends for the lavish parties he gave. Luke's list of woes might easily have alarmed Francis' sensitive spirit.

As well, Luke's version (6:20) of the first Beatitude *(Blessed are you who are poor, for yours is the kingdom of heaven)* may have had more influence on Francis than did Matthew's (5:3) version *(Blessed are the poor in spirit, for theirs is the kingdom of heaven).* Francis felt the need to become *materially* poor for his own spiritual life to flourish. The "less" of poverty was foundational for Francis if he was to lead a life "more" aligned with the kingdom of heaven.

Since Matthew has a longer list of Beatitudes, however, we will employ his version to explore the usefulness of Francis' way for us for today.

The need to mourn

*Blessed are those who mourn, for they will
be comforted* (Matthew 5:4).

We usually associate "mourning" with grieving the loss
of a loved one. Yet we can also mourn about other important
losses like missed opportunities, unfulfilled potential or
wasted gifts. Francis mourned his earlier life of selfishness
because it prevented him from experiencing God's nearness
and love. After tasting the joyful experience of God's presence, he continued to mourn about the way life's distractions
and trivialities hindered movement towards God.

So much for the "less" side of this Beatitude. On the
"more" side we read that mourners will be comforted. Since
mourning and repentance are often connected, the nature of
this comforting is not so obvious. If we are mourning over
losses stemming from our own behaviour, then the comforting we seek will be the experience of God's forgiveness and
healing. From the very beginning, Christians have believed
that being forgiven is the greatest comfort that frail human
nature can ask of God.

Excessive guilt is not a healthy human feeling. In fact, it
can destroy the human personality. On the other hand, we
cannot seek a cure if we do not know we are ill. The great
Jesuit theologian, Karl Rahner, warned that we cannot dis-
pense with guilt as some modern psychologists have sug-
gested. To do so, says Rahner, would be to block off the
desire for forgiveness and healing. Without feeling some
measure of guilt, we cannot feel the need for God's forgiveness. In our efforts to reduce human suffering by minimizing
the importance of guilt, we may have lost something of
immeasurable therapeutic value. If we are once again allowed
to mourn the losses incurred by our own ego-centred behaviour, then the road to change and recovery may be shortened,
via God's forgiveness and healing. A bad infection seldom
heals without proper medication; left unattended it can kill!

Francis' conversion experience began with a long mourning period after his plans for military honour and glory were dashed. But the many months of melancholy gave way to a break with the past that allowed him to pursue a new spiritual direction. Francis humbly laid his sorrows before God and acknowledged his sinfulness, especially his preoccupation with seeking his own glory. He did not mourn his failed projects; rather, he mourned the misguided motivation that had led to these glory-seeking projects. In seeking God's forgiveness and healing grace, Francis' turned his life in the opposite direction, from self-aggrandizement to self-denial

Be less

Blessed are the meek, for they shall inherit the earth (Matthew 5:5).

Other versions or translations have spoken of the "gentle" or the "lowly" rather than the "meek." These three words have similar meanings, but the words "meek" or "lowly" have become offensive in some circles. Women, for instance, no longer want meekness held up to them as a female virtue. Indigenous peoples and other minority groups also find this concept problematic when they are proclaiming the need to preserve their unique cultural heritage. When meekness is imposed, even psychologically, on one group or person by another who is more powerful, there is injustice and victimization. This has nothing to do with the meekness or lowliness or gentleness that Christ advocated.

Franciscans, as we know, use the initials O.F.M. after their names, indicating that they belong to the Order of Friars Minor. In this respect they have preserved the wishes of their founder to the letter. Francis wanted his group of friars to be minors (or "lessers") rather than greaters. He wanted to start a different kind of order that possessed nothing, not even learning, or the beans for tomorrow's dinner.

We may chuckle at the naïvete of these early ideals, but let us give credit where it is due. Maybe Francis had looked carefully ("made an in-depth analysis") at religious life in the Church of his time and seen how very easy it was to start off with great intentions about using money and property for the love of God and neighbour, and to end up somewhere else. Was Francis totally naive, or was he, instead, among the most forward-thinking and courageous persons of his time for daring to say yes to "Blessed are the meek"?

When we look at what Jesus said about our being the light of the world and the salt of the earth, it should be impossible to misinterpret the virtue of meekness as a false humility that prevents us from actualizing our potential as children of God. "Let your light shine before others, so that they may see your good works and give glory to your Father in heaven" (Matthew 5:14). To be meek is to seek God's glory rather than our own, by using the talents and gifts God has given us.

Treat others as God would

Blessed are those who hunger and thirst for righteousness, for they will be filled (Matthew 5:6).

Does meekness mean staying away from justice issues? Not if this Beatitude is observed! At least six different English translations of the Bible use the verbs "hunger and thirst" to describe the true disciple's fervent desire for righteousness or justice (*Jerusalem Bible:* "what is right"). To hunger and thirst are strong feelings. They are cravings for food and drink – those things we need for survival.

Often, the beatitude about meekness is understood as forbidding anger. Nothing could be further from the truth, as this beatitude about righteousness demonstrates. Righteousness reminds us of the possibility of "righteous indignation." Every day news reports present us with cases of exploitation and victimization. What is the appropriate Christian response? As people of compassion we want to alleviate suffering. And as people of intelligence, we want to avoid meaningless short-term solutions, so we go deeper and ask why this or that evil is occurring and how it can be stopped. But we need to go deeper and remember the words of the Brazilian bishop Dom Helder Camara. His famous statement about the dangers of asking why bears repeating here: "When I give food to the poor, they call me a saint; when I ask why the poor have no food, they call me a Communist."

Francis did not ask publicly why the poor were poor, or why the rich tended to be indifferent towards them, or why it seemed so difficult to love God when we also loved many other things. But the depth of his conversion, and the degree of change it brought to his life, suggest that he had grappled with such issues. But for reasons about which we can only speculate, he chose to remain largely silent about the injustices he perceived. Keeping our historical perspective we must recall that the fires of the Inquisition were already burning and a favourite kindling material was outspoken critics of society. In hungering and thirsting primarily to live righteously himself, Francis likely left behind a more insistent focus on the plight of the oppressed than those whose more blatant efforts to alleviate that misery caused conflict and controversy. Clearly Francis' response, like all historical wisdom, must be set in the context of his times.

To hunger and thirst is an experience of "less." We feel the lack of something important. Jesus is saying that those who feel this lack are blessed. When he promises that they will be "filled," we must bear in mind Francis' overall concern to leave empty that which we want God to fill.

In fact, here as elsewhere, Jesus implies the Christian golden rule that we ought to treat others as we would like

God to treat us. The next Beatitude is a straightforward example of this attitude.

Show mercy

Blessed are the merciful, for they will receive mercy (Matthew 5:7).

Through Jesus, God lived out the ultimate act of mercy by becoming one with humankind, an act which ultimately led to the cross. The secular wisdom that recommends "walk a mile in my moccasins" understands that we should not judge others because we are not fully aware of the burdens they carry. Instead of judging, Christians are called to be merciful so that they in turn can receive mercy.

Francis' attitude to the poor and suffering was also to become one with them. By choosing to "walk in their shoes" for the rest of his life, he poured out his own life in mercy and compassion. In spite of this, he so often expressed the unworthiness he felt in light of God's abundant mercy. He knew the disparity was great between his own meagre efforts to love others, and God's overwhelming gift of merciful grace towards his own failings. This awareness kept him ever humble and striving for greater purity of heart.

Walk the straight and narrow

Blessed are the pure in heart, for they will see God (Matthew 5:8).

This Beatitude offers as the "more" the greatest and only prize that Francis and other holy men and women have sought: to see God. On the surface, this one seems to have no "less" side to it. Seeing God and being pure in heart both sound so positive. But to be pure in heart is very much related to walking the straight and narrow path. To be pure is to be free of anything that taints or corrupts. To be pure in heart is to be single-minded in pursuit of holiness or righteousness or God.

Even to be a parent, a role God partakes of and therefore surely approves, is to compromise purity of heart. We love our children, for example, with such a fierce loyalty that we cannot stand before God and claim to have no other real loves at the centre of our hearts. Or perhaps we love spouses or friends or our work with great zeal and fervour. When we look at an "old-fashioned" saint like Francis, who put himself through quite a bit of misery to remain unattached to others and to things, we shake our heads in amazement, and perhaps even disapproval.

But Francis was on fire with the desire to see God, and Jesus had made it clear that purity of heart was necessary to see God. Like the person who sold everything to purchase the pearl of greatest value (Matthew 13:45, 46), Francis was willing to forego all his previous pleasures and preoccupations to open himself to the beatific vision of God. Seeing God was, in fact, the pearl of incomparable value.

Does this mean that our own deep loves and loyalties are detrimental to our pursuit of the spiritual life? No, not at all, since the second commandment – to love others – is so closely connected to the first: to "love the Lord your God with all your heart, and with all your soul, and with all your strength, and with all your mind" (Luke 10:27). Francis' approach contains a valuable message for us. It stresses that our love of others must ultimately lead back to God, so that we, too, may see God.

Live in harmony with others

Blessed are the peacemakers, for they will be called children of God (Matthew 5:9).

If living harmoniously with others were not important, we would not find this previous Beatitude on our list. The last part of Francis' "Canticle to Brother Sun" was added on at a later date. Lines like "Happy those who endure in peace" referred specifically to an explosive local situation involving noblemen or civic authorities. But the concern to diffuse tense situations was hardly new to him. Francis was known as a person of peace, as we see from the "peace prayer" so fondly attached to his memory. But this does not mean that he felt no tensions or disagreements in his life. Many of the early sources, for example, repeatedly mention Francis' admonition to his friars to avoid saying anything critical to or about the local parish priests whose approval was required before a friar could preach in that vicinity. Certain petty jealousies and vested interests seemed to cause considerable grief to friars on fire with the desire to share their vision of God's goodness with others. It was hard to program or put off this sharing until an arbitrarily appointed time, or forever. So Francis was absolutely insistent that the priests were not to be criticized.

The call to be peacemakers does not always mean avoiding conflict. Clearly, if we hunger and thirst for righteousness, we cannot avoid conflict.

Conflict is inevitable

Blessed are those who are persecuted for righteousness' sake, for theirs is the kingdom of heaven (Matthew 5:10).

Whenever we dare to stand up for what is right, we court the anger of those who feel threatened by our actions or words. Yes, we are not to judge, and yes, we are called to be peacemakers, but situations persist that demand our crossing over the line between being popular and serving God. When innocent and relatively powerless people are being victimized by oppressors, when a subtle evil disguised as a good is wreaking havoc in some sector of society, or when values related to

Christ's mandate to love are being attacked or destroyed – do we dare remain silent so people will continue to like us? As the eighteenth-century British philosopher, Edmund Burke, said, "The only thing necessary for the triumph of evil is for good [people] to do nothing." While striving always to be peacemakers, then, we must not allow this ideal to become an excuse for avoiding conflict and an opening for opting out of our responsibilities towards others.

A simple example can be drawn from the delightful experience of parenting teenagers. If we smiled and agreed to all of our teenagers' requests, the typical family home would *appear* to be much more peaceful – no noisy arguments, slamming doors and so on. But underneath this surface harmony, what would we have? For one thing, we would probably be condoning a type of character development in our teenager that is not at all in keeping with Christian ideals of compassion and responsibility. If we want our children eventually to enter the world as mature and capable adults, we dare not duck our own responsibility to pull in the reins when needed, even though this causes us both pain.

The "less" of being persecuted in the cause of right is clear; however, the experience of the "more" – admission to God's kingdom – often seems too distant to matter. But we must witness to the One who has been there and come back to tell about it – to Jesus who lived out this last beatitude fully and passionately. When our strength wavers, we need only to look at the cross to remember that God understands.

Francis endured much ridicule for choosing the way of poverty and humility. His sanity was questioned, and, even as his popularity grew, many parents hid their sons and daughters from his view for fear that their children too would catch this dread disease which caused so many young people to turn their backs on all that their parents had worked to establish. The way of Francis was a basically vagabond existence; in some ways it foreshadowed the "hippie" movement of the 1960s. Though the motivations and goals of each movement were entirely different, mothers and fathers, then and now, could hardly be blamed for trying to prevent their children's total rejection of their values.

Francis' life was not lacking in persecution. For example, his own brother supposedly chided certain friends to "get Francis to sell you a penny's worth of his sweat." And the response of Clare's enraged family when she stole away from the family home to join Francis' movement was not exactly ecstatic or even subtle. Although Francis hated hostility and discord, he was not afraid to embrace and live the last beatitude: *Blessed are you when people revile you and persecute you and utter all kinds of evil against you falsely on my account. Rejoice and be glad, for your reward is great in heaven, for in the same way they persecuted the prophets who were before you* (Matthew 5:11, 12).

The Beatitudes are indeed a paradox. They call us to be gentle and meek and merciful and peacemakers; but, at the same time, they also call us to be strong and bold and fearless in the face of the persecution that often results from authentic Christian living. The Beatitudes promise us *more* joy and peace in the future if we live with *less* comfort and popularity now. We need only look at Francis' life — an inner acceptance of privation and persecution co-existed with an outward joy, for which he is remembered so fondly. After all, that is the final instruction of the Beatitudes: "Rejoice and be glad!"

5

The ecumenical question

In the last few decades, different Christian denominations have tried to approach one another with a new level of love and respect. Although the differences are real, inter-denominational dialogue has exposed surprisingly broad areas of agreement on matters of church doctrine and belief, as well as in approaches to the Bible and the sacraments. Realistically speaking, complete rapprochement is still only a distant dream. But a huge hurdle has been overcome: respect and openness towards each other is the most common attitude among Christian denominations today.

Can Francis of Assisi offer anything of relevance to this modern attempt at Christian convergence? I believe he can offer us much, even though one can hardly expect quotable ecumenical quotes from a person who lived three hundred years before the Reformation! Francis belongs to all Christians because he was a product of that common Christian heritage that predates the separation of western Christianity into various expressions. In fact, his desire to rid life and faith of non-essentials makes him a model Christian for all denominations and a shining example to non-Christians of what it means to be a true follower of Christ.

Although the term ecumenical usually refers to inter-Christian dialogue, there is clearly a need to demonstrate this attitude of respectful openness to faith communities outside the purely Christian realm. Inter-religious dialogue recognizes that we live in a pluralistic world with many deep-rooted religious traditions. Increasingly, we are coming to see that all religions share certain truths and concerns about life and destiny. To the extent that we can glimpse these truths, we can bring greater harmony to the world.

Francis saw that intimacy with God required as uncluttered a life as possible. His desire to be rid of non-essentials led him into extended prayer vigils and retreats in the secluded hills of his native Assisi. In solitary reflection and prayer, he sought to fill the gnawing emptiness of his being with something substantial. He eventually came to see that ignorance and desire had marred his past life. Desiring popularity and sensual pleasures, he had remained ignorant of God's offer of a more blissful life, the life of the disciple.

I have often been struck by the similarities between what Francis taught and what the Buddha taught. Buddhism is a religion of great compassion for human suffering. Francis, too, like Prince Gautama, the founder of Buddhism, was so moved by the reality of human misery that he could no longer remain in his sheltered earlier life. Both these men sought a life of greater purity. And both were moved to strip away the non-essentials that cluttered up the life of the spirit.

I believe we can deepen our understanding of Francis' relevance for today by pursuing the comparison a little further. If Francis is a saint worthy of our attention in the twenty-first century, we must consider how his vision compares with that of the Buddha, another master of the spiritual life.

At the centre of Buddhist teaching we find the eightfold path, Buddha's way of dealing with the spiritual obstacles of "desire" and "ignorance." To understand even better Francis' relevance for today, I now want to look at how his "way" compares with the Buddhist eightfold "path" which dates back five centuries before Christ. If Francis' way has much in common with an important non-Christian teaching like the eightfold path, then our reasons for carrying him into the twenty-first century, as model and mentor, are enhanced. By following Francis we can follow Christ more closely; and we can be more open towards the wisdom contained in other faiths.

The eightfold path, in skeletal form, is as follows:
1) right views
2) right aspirations
3) right speech
4) right conduct
5) right mode of living
6) right effort
7) right awareness
8) right concentration

Right views

The Buddhist disciple begins by trying to take on the "right views" that the Buddha himself would have endorsed as a person of infinite compassion for the sufferings of others. Perhaps we could describe "right views" as a proper perspective, or a good point of departure.

The first beatitude asserts that the poor (or poor in spirit) are blessed. Poverty, Francis emphatically agreed, gives us a unique perspective. As a young adult, Francis' conversion was profound; his view of the world changed dramatically. Perhaps this is why a period of confusion bordering on despair often precedes conversion experiences. The outlook that previously made sense of the world no longer explains anything; the point of view that used to work automatically seems to stop functioning. Our view is clouded. We look at the world, we look at the places in our lives that used to bring comfort and joy – all is empty. We pray then for sight and insight. We pray for the right understanding of what is important in life and what is not.

Psalm 19 beautifully praises both God's works and God's law. Both bring delight and nurture. But no one's perspective is entirely unflawed. That's why the psalm continues: "But who can detect their errors? Clear me from hidden faults" (Psalm 19:12). Francis was a happy, carefree and generous youth. He probably loved God as much as the average person in Assisi did. And he loved the beauty of creation. His outlook, his view of things, seemed to be a very positive one. And yet he came to that crossroads in his spiritual life, that place where the cross of Christ broke into his view of reality and turned everything upside down. He wandered the lonely hills of Assisi and took refuge in their womb-like caves. There a new view of reality came to him, one that shone with the suffering love of the Saviour – the "right view" that Jesus himself lived.

Right aspirations

Francis' immediate concern then was what to do. With his new view of reality, with the crucified Christ at its centre, towards what should he be aspiring? Here he was, weak, penniless, humiliated and homeless – for what should he be aiming?

We all need goals in life, a sense of purpose and direction. We need "right aspirations." What should we be trying to accomplish? What should we be hoping to achieve? The Christian beatitude that blesses the peacemakers is an obvious example of a right aspiration. With our energies focussed on establishing God's reign on earth, we can aspire towards reducing hate and misunderstanding in our world.

As a person of peace, Francis aspired to a life of harmony with God, other people, animals and the earth. Modern Christians, who might find Francis entirely too silent about the corruption in the Church of his time, might bear in mind that Francis nurtured a strong aspiration to preserve peace as much as possible. As the current millennium draws to a close, we find ourselves especially oriented towards the future. And as people of faith, this might be a suitable time to refocus on God's Kingdom and on our aspirations to see it more fully revealed in our midst.

Right speech

Francis, in the third beatitude's spirit of meekness, said very little to anyone at first about his new view of reality and his gradually unfolding understanding of the role he was to play. His first followers were not at all "talked into" joining. Rather they were attracted, almost magnetically, to Francis' largely silent task of repairing the church of San Damiano. Many early biographies attest to Francis' reluctance to speak. He was aware of his lack of education; but, even more than this, he was convinced of his insignificance and general worthlessness and sinfulness. At the same time he knew that God could make very good use of him, *if* God chose to do so, and *if* Francis could keep up his vigilant guard against the personal pride that had previously dictated most of his thoughts and actions. Eventually Francis became known as a great preacher; but, even after his reputation was well established, there were times when he remained silent in front of a waiting crowd because he did not hear the Holy Spirit giving him any message at that moment. If Francis could not give the "right speech," the one from God, then he preferred to give no speech.

Right speech is the third step on the Buddhist's eightfold path. Unfortunately "wrong speech" seems to be the order of the day. We are bombarded with words, both spoken and written, and this is having an extremely negative effect on our capacity to react. Many researchers have shown the numbness with which the TV generation tends to greet images of new human suffering. Overexposure to painful realities has had an inoculation effect: we no longer react!

The computer is also a wonderful tool, absolutely stunning in its potential for bringing language and communication to a new plateau of excellence. But, like television, it can also dull our creative faculties. Since it can do so much for us (spell checks, grammar verification and so forth), it plays on the human tendency to look for lazy shortcuts. Beautiful looking text is no substitute for adequate reflection and serious engagement with the topic at hand.

Dag Hammarskjold, the profoundly Christian former Secretary General of the United Nations, and a person much concerned to use language well as an instrument of world peace, wrote in his diary called *Markings:* "Respect for the word – to employ it with scrupulous care and an incorruptible heart-felt love of truth – is essential if there is to be any growth in a society or a human race. To misuse the word is to show contempt for man. It undermines the bridge and poisons the wells. It causes man to regress down the long path of his evolution. 'But I say unto you, that every idle word that men speak . . .'" (London: Faber & Faber, 1964, p. 101). I believe Hammarskjold is correct. He is not just exaggerating with poetic metaphors. Truly, the misuse of the word does undermine the bridges and poison the wells. When we become slovenly in our use of language, we undermine the bridges that link one person to another because we fail to attach sufficient importance to communicating well. And we poison the wells that water the seed of God's word when we say that right speech doesn't matter so long as we fill every minute with a variety of sounds, instead of waiting in the silence for the words of the Spirit, as Francis did.

Let us join with Francis in realizing the importance of right speech in the midst of a noisy world.

Right conduct

We might align this fourth step on the Buddhist eightfold path with Christ's beatitude that blesses the merciful and promises that they shall obtain mercy. Being merciful towards others means always allowing for their genuine needs and meeting their failings with ready forgiveness. Every person is equally precious and equally a candidate for the enjoyment of eternal life. Therefore we dare not treat others as inferior or count their needs as insignificant.

Buddhists place great value on a life of quiet. Even to move a chair noisily is frowned upon. This resonates well with Francis who loved to be alone in the quiet and beauty of nature. He was clearly a person of peace, solitude and depth. Since the advent of affordable electronic music-playing devices, our own affluent society seems to have forgotten the good manners or "right conduct" of keeping our noise from disturbing the silent journeys of the souls of others. A society that encourages a "me-first" attitude cannot hope to see its citizens conduct themselves in considerate ways.

Good manners are considered old-fashioned. And many of the trivial rules of etiquette are just that – trivial. But the overall attitude of genuine good manners, the attitude that literally and figuratively bows to the needs of the other, is an attitude worth preserving in a society claiming to be civilized. Francis always considered the other to be greater than he. He sought, in today's jargon, neither to "keep up" with the Joneses nor to "one-up" them. Instead he sought always to have less prestige and possessions than anyone else. His stance may have been extreme, but the modern insatiability for "more" suggests an extreme in the other direction.

Right mode of living

Francis adopted a lifestyle that removed all distractions from his goal of seeing God. For Francis, material poverty was necessary for a "right mode of living." Physical austerity seemed to leave more space for spiritual joy. The idea is not new; it's called asceticism and belongs to most of the great religious traditions of human history, including Buddhism. This "right mode of living" refers to a lifestyle free from luxury. In this, one is reminded of Christ's beatitude in favour of those who mourn. If those who mourn are blessed and will be comforted by God, then no doubt Francis and the Buddha were right in rejecting so many earthly comforts in favour of spiritual ones.

Upward mobility and conspicuous consumption have been the guiding principles of our society in the last few decades. Certainly no popularity contests are won by those who claim that downward mobility and conspicuous austerity are more in keeping with spiritual pursuits. The simple fact that we must leave space in our lives for God seems to have been continually overshadowed by human material pursuits. The time has come for a renewed asceticism (a "neo-asceticism") that rejects consumerism and embraces the purity and joy of a simpler life. It's been a century and a half since Thoreau wrote of these simple but enduring truths in *Walden*. Such a mode of living is surely right – and more ecologically responsible as well. Perhaps caring for our souls and caring for the earth have more in common than we suspected.

Right effort

Our "effort" is the work we do, especially our work as disciples. As disciples of Christ we know that people who hunger and thirst for what is right are blessed. Our efforts, then, should reflect this hunger and thirst for righteousness. Francis hungered, above all, for God. His other efforts were aimed mostly at crushing that which distracted him from this goal.

The conscientious modern Christian is called to expend effort in so many worthwhile directions. Modern communications make vast areas of human need and suffering so present to our lives. The media have opened up potential areas requiring the practice of "right effort." Neither Francis nor the Buddha had this experience of being electronically aware of so much bad news. But they lived lives that carefully balanced the needs of others *and* the care of their own spirit, and their example of right effort remains valid.

Right awareness

St. Ignatius of Loyola called it discernment. This seventh step of the eightfold path is akin to God's gift of wisdom. We need the discernment born of wisdom to experience right awareness. But how can we become wise? Wisdom is not simply knowledge or information that can be learned from a course or a book. St. Paul tells us that God's foolishness is wiser than human wisdom (1 Corinthians 1:25). Enter St. Francis – God's fool.

The way of St. Francis is fraught with foolishness according to the world's standards. Francis was foolishly joyful for no reason except that he took delight in the love of the living God. Francis was foolishly generous to the point of giving away his only cloak or his last bit of food. Francis was foolishly trusting, able to ignore the rejection of so many of the worldly wise while he threw himself with total abandon on the mercy and goodness of God.

Right awareness is the wisdom of seeing the possibilities for blessedness in every situation including, or perhaps especially in, situations of disappointment or sorrow. We often hear stories of how well someone has coped with a trying situation. And then we see others who become quite frustrated or even despairing over problems that are relatively minor. So much seems to depend on one's attitude.

The final beatitude tells us that people persecuted for righteousness' sake are blessed. The notion that authentic discipleship leads to the cross is not a popular one. Yet being aware of this fact may help us to endure the unavoidable trials that come when we accept Christ's mandate to love. Francis accepted the life of the cross. He accepted privation and sorrow and, in so doing, opened himself to the eternal delight that comes with the "right awareness" of God's nearness and love.

Right concentration

The final step towards the cessation of suffering on the Buddhist eightfold path is "right concentration." We can compare this concentration to the contemplative solace of retreat and prayer, leading to the purity of heart extolled in the Beatitudes. Following Jesus' example, Francis often left his leadership duties behind for a brief and solitary sojourn in some quiet, out-of-the-way place. As it was with Jesus, so it was with Francis: rejection gave way to a near insatiability for the presence of this holy man. As people began to hear the stories of Jesus' holiness they clamoured for more of his time and attention. But even Jesus needed to get away once in a while to pray. Francis, and every other great saint, had the same need.

We, too, must step back from our busy lives, even if we are doing the Lord's work. Like the apostles who rejoined Jesus after being sent out to work, we must come back and offer to the Lord the fruit or, in some cases, the frustrations, of our labour. Then Jesus said to the apostles, as he says to us: "Come away to a deserted place all by yourselves and rest a while" (Mark 6:31).

* * *

In using the eightfold path to highlight Francis' continued relevance, and in hinting at its affinity with the Beatitudes, I wanted to show that great spiritual minds think alike. As Christians we revere above all Christ's teachings and examples. As people secure in our faith we need not fear that the truth of Christianity will be threatened by the truth of other great faiths. Great truths do not diminish one another; rather, they enhance one another. Though not living in an ecumenical or pluralistic age like our own, Francis, by concentrating on the essentials, is a model that can help us be more open to other faith expressions.

6

Integrating
the negative

Many people will never pick up this or any other book about a saint because they feel quite uncomfortable with the notion of sainthood. Since saints were such holy and virtuous people, many an ordinary mortal feels either intimidated by or contemptuous of these faith heroes with their apparently superhuman ability to do good and avoid evil.

In every religious tradition, legends grow up that exaggerate a saint's good qualities and reduce or even eliminate his or her flaws and foibles. These tall tales are not the result of a malicious intent to deceive; rather, they reflect a faith community's fervent gratitude and admiration for this person. As well, the biographer may have had a particular "axe to grind" and decided that the saint would be a fitting oracle for this or that important issue.

In other words, different stories about the saints might contain some unreliable details. They may even contradict each other. And, the more popular the saint, the more numerous the stories, and the more likely these stories are not equally believable.

Perhaps the greatest danger is one that seems most benign – the danger of making the saint look too holy. Many people become skeptical and lose interest in such individuals. Perfect characters belong in the comics or in fairy tales. Always being tolerant and charitable and wise and other-centred and good is not easy, as any adult knows. Following the dictates of the ego, on the other hand, often seems less difficult. What would the saints know about this, we wonder, when they were so perfect and holy and good?

Particularly annoying in this regard are saints who apparently craved nothing but closeness to God from their earliest childhood to the moment of their last breath. They may be valuable in heaven, but they have so little in common with us ordinary mortals that we shrug our shoulders with indifference. What's the point in comparing their spotless lives with our highly imperfect ones?

Francis' conversion was at least preceded by years of vain self-indulgence and of very human cravings for personal fame and glory. To believe that Francis was never again seriously plagued by temptations of the ego after his vision at San Damiano and subsequent conversion is to overlook both the height of his ultimate heroism and the depth of the common human frailty he continued to experience. Francis never turned his back on the ongoing challenge of what it means to be human.

Integrating the negative

As Brazilian liberation theologian Leonardo Boff explains in his study of Francis, this man did not become a saint by overcoming the negative aspects of human experience; rather, he was able to incorporate these painful negativities into the integrated life of seeking and serving God. Francis never allowed anyone to forget that he and his friars were "minors," or lessers, rather than greaters. They were not closer to perfection than others; they were further away. Because of this, they had to submit to what Boff calls a "terrible asceticism" to avoid being too distracted from the life of faith and service.

Boff understands Francis' attachment to poverty as a deliberate letting go of the will to power, or the desire to dominate. This inner struggle is perhaps even more acute in the saint than in others, since the saint is so sensitive about all that distracts from God. Sanctity, according to Boff, is not a *permanent* state of peaceful and joyful intimacy with God, at least not on this side of the grave: "Behind the saint is hidden a person who has conquered the hells of human nature and the crush of sins, despair, and the denial of God. They have fought with God like Jacob (Genesis 23) and they have been marked by the battle. Because of this it is foolish and unthinking to imagine the life of a saint as carefree, easy, and clear-cut. Sainthood is a reward for a painful battle that has been won."[1]

In our own attempts at greater fidelity to Christ's gospel, we endure many painful battles. The gospels call us to Christ's example of self-sacrifice. Our contemporary culture, on the other hand, often preys on our human weakness for what is "carefree, easy and clear-cut." We feel pushed and pulled – pushed towards the "world" and thinking only of "me," and pulled towards Christ and thinking first of "others." This spiritual tug-of-war can be wearying, and following Christ seems to result only in a life of continual strain.

What, I used to wonder, did the saints know about this tension? Surely their lives were as clean and pretty as a well-tended garden? And when a weed grew, some nasty thought or greedy urge, the superior faith of the saint would pull it out, root and all, and throw it on the fire. Not like me, I

---

1. Leonardo Boff. *Saint Francis: A Model for Human Liberation.* (New York: Crossroad, 1989), p. 131.

thought, whose "garden" is so overgrown with the weeds of recurring pettiness and misspent gifts that the cultivated plants of virtuous living are all but buried and choked. But Francis, according to Boff, was always pulling weeds. The garden of his spiritual life was planted on the rocky ground of his typical human flaws and temptations.

Francis' experience of grace was not just an experience of ecstatic bliss. "If it feels good, do it" – this is the "wisdom" of the modern age. Francis clearly did not agree. In fact, he did many things that felt uncomfortable because they seemed necessary for the grace of God's presence to flow.

Francis may have been uneducated but he was no simpleton. His understanding of God's presence in human life has much in common with Karl Rahner's, who described the experience of grace in this way: "Have we ever kept quiet, even though we wanted to defend ourselves when we had been unfairly treated? Have we ever forgiven someone even though we got no thanks for it? . . . Have we ever sacrificed something without receiving any thanks or recognition for it, and even without a feeling of inner satisfaction? Have we ever been absolutely lonely? Have we ever decided on some course of action . . . taking a decision which no one else can take in one's place and for which one will have to answer for all eternity? . . . Have we ever tried to love God when we seemed to be calling out into emptiness and our cry seemed to fall on deaf ears . . . ?"[2]

Though known for the complexity of his theological thought, here Rahner gives us a simple and beautiful description of the grace experience. Yet it is difficult to recommend this to others. In the past, minority groups, enslaved people and women in general were often admonished by teachers and pastors to be "lowly and obedient" as Christ was. Ironically, these same pastors and teachers followed a very

---

2.   Karl Rahner. *Theological Investigations.* Vol. 3. (New York: Crossroad, 1982), p. 87.

different path, one that involved grabbing and using power to suppress differences. True, as St. Paul says, there are a variety of gifts; but who among us can command the Holy Spirit to restrict certain gifts to certain people?

We are all called to experience the kind of grace that Karl Rahner describes – to translate our moments of loneliness, failure and fear into times when our hunger for God is greatest. This is to integrate the negative – to turn life's inevitable pains and frustrations into avenues of grace.

"Taste and see that the Lord is Good." When we are full, even a sumptuous meal fails to excite. When we have been emptied of our pretensions, and separated from our various security blankets, the Spirit has room to work and to touch our lives with a delicious awareness of God's presence and love. Here is a reflection on one such moment in my own life:

> Lord, you have made me giddy with joy and love,
>   laughter, friends, peace and hope.
> Deserving nothing, knowing my shallowness,
>   knowing how many things of the world
>   command my heart and caring,
> I am struck, overwhelmed, in awe,
>   at the immensity of your gifts,
>   outpouring tender love and grace.
> Like the saints of old,
>   I long to touch your nearness.
> You are great beyond the greatness of princes,
>   you are wise beyond all learning,
>   you are the arms of friends wrapped around me,
>   the glint in their eyes that speaks love
>   more clearly than words.
> I know there is pain in neighbouring houses,
>   towns and countries . . .
> I know there is pain in my past,
>   and will be in my future,

But just for now,
     just for this grace-filled present moment,
I choose to believe that nothing exists
     beyond this cherished embrace.

Francis drew tremendous strength from his cherished moments of encounter with the living God. He remained available both to his fellow Franciscans and to the world of lay people at large. He did not shun the world to maintain some kind of pristine contact with God. Instead, he accepted the negativities of contact with the world along with the simple hardships of being fully human – he accepted and celebrated the abundant grace with which God met the heavily burdened pilgrim: "Come to me, all you that are . . . carrying heavy burdens, and I will give you rest" (Matthew 11:28).

To portray Francis the saint as having overcome life's negative aspects once and for all is to do him and ourselves a disservice. When St. Paul speaks of his frustration at God for not removing the "thorn in the flesh" once and for all, he writes: "I appealed to the Lord about this, that it would leave me, but he said to me, 'My grace is sufficient for you, for power is made perfect in weakness . . . .' Therefore I am content with weaknesses, insults, hardships, persecutions and calamities for the sake of Christ; for whenever I am weak, then I am strong" (2 Corinthians 12:8-10).

The invitation to follow Francis and, through Francis, Christ, is an invitation to grow through our challenges, trials and frustrations. We are invited to make our way in the real world, not in an artificial paradise where negativities do not exist. And we are invited to be lesser brothers and sisters that we might grow as persons and as children of God.

Conclusion

A fire burned in the heart of Francis of Assisi, the fire of his passionate desire to walk always in the full awareness of God's presence. To take delight in the living God was his lifelong passion and mission. And he looked to all God's creatures, indeed to all of creation, to "Sister Earth," for a clearer view of this Creator and Redeemer and Advocate whom he loved.

For the Christian, Christ is the supreme incarnation of the living God. There are many names for God in many different cultural settings. And many heroes of faith in many different religious traditions have enhanced people's awareness of God's nearness and love.

St. Paul, for example, writing during the first century after Christ's death, called all Christians "saints." For Paul, to follow the way, the truth and the life of Christ was to invite the Spirit of God to dwell within our hearts and lives.

Twelve centuries later, a young man named Francesco Bernardone heard the call of Christ so clearly that it turned his whole life upside down. Francis' rebirth into Christ was a painful process involving the giving up of many sensual pleasures in favour of spiritual ones. At first, Francis' family and friends considered him deluded, not inspired. His father apparently never changed his opinion – a fact which no doubt contributed to Francis' ongoing heartache in spite of his deeply rooted joyfulness in Christ.

Francis taught and wrote very little in a formal way. But he chose, as Henry David Thoreau put it, to march to the beat of a different drummer. Though religious orders for men abounded in thirteenth-century Assisi, he took the risk of insisting to the pope himself that his was a radically new way of being faithful to Christ, a way that could not be accommodated in the established orders of the time. And the pope, after first rejecting the idea, was inspired (by a dream) to see Francis' way as crucial to the Church's continued survival and growth.

For Francis, simplicity, poverty and reverence for creation were the way to ever greater closeness to Christ. As the Franciscan order grew, it became increasingly difficult to live as simply as Francis wished. However, today's concern for the health of the environment gives Francis' way a renewed relevance. For those who care about the environment and love the Creator from whom all natural wonders flow, ecology is also a sacred issue. Who could be a better model than Francis of Assisi, who never ceased to take delight in the creation that manifested the greatness of the Creator?

Our world is beset with numerous social problems as well. In our relatively well-to-do society, we have increasing violence, crime and interpersonal alienation. We can no longer pretend that greed and self-centredness are unrelated to excessive consumerism. By rejecting excessive consumerism, we reject the envies and fears that come with material preoccupations; and we free up our spirits to celebrate life and each other more. Any kind of rampant consumerism is the antithesis of Francis' way. Francis found that dependency on money and things did not allow him to experience the immense spiritual freedom that Christ had promised us. By refusing to be weighed down by many possessions, Francis was "light enough" in spirit to give himself totally to Christ.

Anyone who makes this total gift of self soon recalls Christ's thrice-repeated question to Peter: "Do you love me?" And, after being reassured of the disciple's love, Christ's thrice-repeated instruction: "Feed my sheep." What exactly did Christ mean? Each century since his time has produced countless volumes of theological reflection on that question. Clearly, I cannot give a comprehensive answer here. But, one thing is clear: human beings need both physical and spiritual food. To focus on one to the exclusion of the other is unhealthy.

Francis chose to share all he had with those in need and to live like the poorest of the poor. Distancing himself from all forms of luxury, he adopted a lifestyle that left his spirit free for Christ and resources available for the alleviation of poverty.

Sensing his affinity with his fellow creatures, the animals, the earth and all its elements, Francis always refrained from causing them harm. He taught by example that all of creation was an aspect of the Creator to whom we owe our lives and sustenance. This teaching gave abundant nourishment to the sheep of the flock.

Will we have the courage today to follow "Il Poverello" (the little poor one) of Assisi who, as one of humankind's truly great teachers, pointed out a better way? Following the way of Francis would both free our spiritual lives from unnecessary and distracting clutter and guide us in the ongoing liberation of all our fellow creatures, human and non-human, with whom we share the planet.

The spirit of Francis was a fire, the "brother" through whom he praised God in his canticle. Francis also looked to his "sister," the earth, not only to show him the glory of the Creator, but to receive his body at life's end, so that his spirit might fly unfettered to be with its beloved. Describing his initial fears after attracting a few followers, Francis wrote in his Testament: "There was no one to tell me what I should do, but the Most High himself made it clear to me that I must live the life of the Gospel." And, by living that life in union with Brother Fire and Sister Earth, this most human of saints has become a model for all those committed to building a socially responsible world.

Suggested reading

Boff, Leonardo. *Saint Francis: A Model for Human Liberation*. Translated by John W. Diercksmeier. New York: Crossroad, 1989.

Francis of Assisi. *Writings and Early Biographies: English Omnibus of Sources for the Life of St. Francis*. Edited by Marion A. Habig. Chicago: Franciscan Herald, 1983.

Hammarskjold, Dag. *Markings*. Translated by W. H. Auden and Leif Sjoberg. London: Faber & Faber, 1964.

Heschel, Abraham Joshua. *Man Is Not Alone: A Philosophy of Religion*. New York: Farrar, Straus & Giroux, 1951.

Kohak, Erazim. *The Embers and the Stars: A Philosophical Inquiry into the Moral Sense of Nature*. Chicago: University of Chicago Press, 1987.

New Revised Standard Version of the Holy Bible. Nashville, Tennessee: Thomas Nelson, Inc., 1989.

Rahner, Karl. *Theological Investigations*. Vol. 3. *(The Theology of the Spiritual Life)*. Translated by Karl-H. and Boniface Kruger. New York: Crossroad, 1982.

Schumacher, E. F. *Small Is Beautiful: A Study of Economics as if People Mattered*. London: Abacus, 1974.

INNER JOURNEY SERIES

BROTHER FIRE, SISTER EARTH
The Way of Francis of Assisi
for a Socially Responsible World

Adela DiUbaldo Torchia

Adela Torchia shows us why Saint Francis is still so very important for anyone trying to remain faithful to Christ's gospel today.
ISBN 2-89088-617-4
80 pages, 5.25 x 8.25 inches, $7.95

HEALING THE HEART
Desert Wisdom for a Busy World

Kenneth C. Russel

Author Kenneth C. Russell has us sit symbolically at the feet of John Cassian, one of the Desert Fathers and spiritual master to ask him, as was customary in the desert, for a "word" by which we might guide our lives today.
ISBN 2-89088-618-2
96 pages, 5.25 x 8.25 inches, $7.95

KNOWING THE GOD OF COMPASSION
Spirituality and Persons Living with AIDS

Richard P. Hardy

Author Richard Hardy lets people with AIDS tell their story; and, in so doing, their way of being religious, their way of coming to know the God of compassion, unfurls before you.
ISBN 2-89088-632-8
80 pages, 5.25 x 8.25 inches, $7.95

TO ORDER

Novalis
49 Front Street East, Second Floor, Toronto, ON M5E 1B3
1 -800-387-7164
Toronto area (416) 363-3303
1-416-363-9409